Hippocrates
Making the Way for Medicine

Connie Jankowski

Life Science Readers:
Hippocrates: Making the Way for Medicine

Publishing Credits

Editorial Director
Dona Herweck Rice

Creative Director
Lee Aucoin

Associate Editor
Joshua BishopRoby

Illustration Manager
Timothy J. Bradley

Editor-in-Chief
Sharon Coan, M.S.Ed.

Publisher
Rachelle Cracchiolo, M.S.Ed.

Science Contributor
Sally Ride Science™

Science Consultants
Thomas R. Ciccone, B.S., M.A.Ed.,
    Chino Hills High School
Dr. Ronald Edwards,
    DePaul University

Teacher Created Materials

5301 Oceanus Drive
Huntington Beach, CA 92649
http://www.tcmpub.com
ISBN 978-0-7439-0596-1

Table of Contents

A Man Ahead of His Time

The field of medicine has seen great men and women. The great ones change the world. They improve lives. They have something in common, too. They use good judgment when making difficult decisions.

Hippocrates (hih-PAHK-ruh-teez) was a Greek doctor. He was also a free thinker. He changed the world of medicine. He had great insights. For this, he is called The Father of Medicine. Until he practiced medicine, there was little science in medicine. Doctors performed rituals they thought would help healing.

Hippocrates' work changed many areas of medicine. He changed the study of the structure of the human body. He changed the study of how the body works. He also changed the study of mental and emotional health.

"Magical" Medicine

Before medicine was developed, people tried to use magic to heal the sick. They thought everything happened because of angry gods or evil spirits. They believed that illness was a punishment from the gods. Surgery was performed to give evil spirits a way to escape. People drilled holes in the head to heal headaches and mental problems!

Erasistratus

Erasistratus (er-uh-SIS-truh-tuhs) was born in Ceos, an island in Greece. He lived from about 330 B.C. to 250 B.C. He was a doctor. He is best known for healing the king's son, who had nervous depression. The prince was in love, but there were things in the way of him being with the one he loved. Erasistratus helped the prince unite with his love. He was healed.

Erasistratus also studied human **anatomy**. He was especially devoted to the **dissection** of the human body. He gave special attention to the nervous system. Due to his skill, he led a medical school in Alexandria.

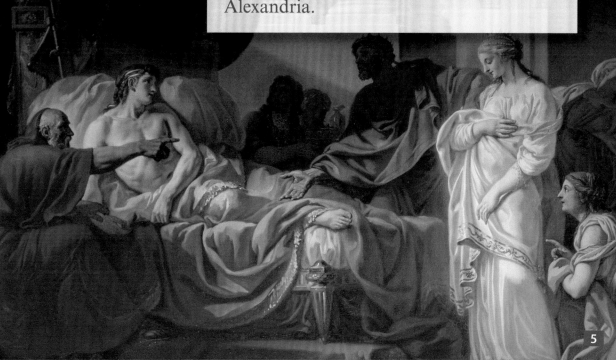

Hippocrates' Early Years

Hippocrates was born on an island called Kos. Kos is in a corner of the Aegean Sea. Hippocrates was born around 460 B.C. He lived for more than 90 years. His work lives on today.

Hippocrates had a pleasant childhood. Like today, children then liked to play. They played many of the same games children play today. Hippocrates had tops, balls, and toy animals as a boy. He also had pet dogs and cats, just as children today might have.

It is believed Hippocrates stayed on the island for his schooling. His studies were divided into two parts. One was physical education and the other was mental discipline. He learned to read, write, and spell. The Greeks believed that this prepared young men for citizenship and leadership.

Greece

Greece is made up of a peninsula and surrounding islands. The climate is mild and pleasant. Greeks long ago and today can farm and fish easily. Because of these qualities, and because of its prime location, Greece became a center for trade and the center of civilization. It was a good place for Hippocrates to study and learn.

Horse Master

Hippocrates is a Greek name. It means "horse master."

Two thousand years ago, people were very superstitious. They thought evil spirits caused illnesses. People would go to temples for help. They asked the god of medicine to help them. They thought the god could heal them. Others would say magic words over the sick person. They thought this would heal them.

Many people in Hippocrates' family were priests and doctors. Hippocrates studied medicine under his father. He became a doctor like his father. He left the island at about age 30.

He moved to the island of Rhodes. He continued to study medicine. The schools were located in healing temples. Each student studied under a doctor. The main way of healing was finding physical peace. They used changes of diet, bathing, and exercise to treat diseases.

Healthy Teeth

Ancient Greeks had little trouble with their teeth. Their diet included very little sugar. They ate a lot of whole-grained foods. They cleaned their teeth with sticks. Because of their diet, their teeth were healthy.

This coin depicts Asklepios, the Greek god of healing.

Florence Nightingale

(1820–1910)

Florence Nightingale is the founder of modern nursing. She was born into a wealthy British family. Her family wanted her to become an obedient wife and mother. Her job would be to care for her husband.

Luckily, she did not follow their wishes. She followed her heart. She traveled the world helping those in need. She went to Germany to study nursing. The experience made her more sure of her choice.

She fought for improved medical care. She fought for better conditions in hospitals. She wrote a thousand-page report for Queen Victoria. It detailed the needs in military medicine. This led to a change in army medical care. It also led to the opening of an Army Medical School. Nightingale also established an early nursing school at St. Thomas Hospital in 1860.

Sir Alexander Fleming
(1881–1955)

Sir Alexander Fleming was born in Scotland and raised on a farm. After school, he worked in a shipping office. When he inherited money, he decided to study medicine. At the age of 20, he went back to school.

Fleming joined the research department of his medical school. He began working with a pioneer in vaccine therapy. During this time, Fleming discovered **penicillin**. It is a drug that has saved millions of lives. Fleming and penicillin have changed the world of medicine. In 1945, Fleming was awarded the **Nobel Prize** for his work.

Hippocrates Changes Medicine

Hippocrates thought there were natural causes for diseases. He didn't think gods caused illnesses. He thought there were internal, personal reasons for them. He tried to explain and find reasons for illness. He thought if you could find the cause, you could find a cure.

He thought the body should be treated as a whole instead of as a bunch of parts. He observed patients. He would pay attention to their symptoms. He would look at the color of their skin. He would look at their eyes. He'd see if they had fevers and chills.

He was the first doctor to describe the symptoms of **pneumonia**. He also described **epilepsy** in children. He accurately described arthritis and mumps. He described other illnesses, as well.

Taking Care of Yourself
You can help take care of yourself, too. You can eat well and exercise. You can get plenty of rest and fresh air. What else can you do?

Hippocrates believed the body contained four **humors**. These fluids were black **bile**, yellow bile, blood, and **phlegm**. He thought these caused people to become ill. Illness would occur when these fluids were unbalanced. Someone would vomit, cough, or sweat. This was the body's way of getting rid of excess amounts of one of these fluids.

Later, doctors would develop better theories, but the four humors got them started. Doctors started to look at science to understand illnesses. They no longer only thought the gods were to blame.

Hippocrates was the first doctor to speak of the need for cleanliness. When the plague broke out, he told people to burn their clothes.

These images depict the imbalance of the four humors.

Heart or Brain?

Hippocrates was the first to think that thoughts and feelings come from the brain. Before him, people thought they came from the heart.

Early Pharmacists

Doctors usually prepared their own medicines for patients. Some trained assistants to handle this chore. The assistants became the first pharmacists. They collected roots and dried them. They ground them and prepared them for patients.

⬆ Hippocrates told the people in cities suffering from plagues to burn their clothes. This got rid of the disease's germs.

Healing Laughter

They say that laughter is the best medicine. Studies show that laughter is actually good for your health! Being unhappy or very sad can ruin your health. But laughing can improve it. Do you know any good jokes?

Hippocrates believed the human body could heal itself. He thought there were simple ways to heal a person. Rest and a good diet were two ways. He also thought fresh air and cleanliness would help. He told his patients to eat well. They shouldn't eat too much or too little. They should exercise. Walking was especially recommended.

Hippocrates wanted doctors to wash their hands before treating patients. He thought doctor's offices and operating rooms should be cheerfully decorated. He believed this would help patients heal quicker.

Hippocrates noticed that some people had the same disease. But that didn't mean they were affected the same. There were different levels of severity to the diseases. Some people could also cope better with their illness.

Louis Pasteur (1822–1895)

Louis Pasteur was born in France into a poor family. He did not do well in school. He preferred to fish and draw. As he got older, though, he became interested in science. He went to college and did well there. He was very curious. This led him to explore many areas of science.

Pasteur made many discoveries. He developed a vaccine to fight rabies. He is best known for finding a way to prevent milk from going sour. This process is called **pasteurization**. It is used on the milk in grocery stores today. It keeps milk and other drinks from spoiling quickly. It prevents related diseases.

Pasteur in his laboratory

Elizabeth Blackwell
(1821–1910)

Elizabeth Blackwell was born in England. Her family was wealthy. They moved to New York City when she was young. As an adult, she became a teacher. She dreamed of being a doctor.

Blackwell applied to several medical schools. She was always rejected. She was finally accepted at Geneva College. The students voted on whether to let her in, but they thought her application was a prank. They accepted her. They never thought she'd appear. She did. She graduated first in her class in 1849. She was the first woman to earn a medical degree in the United States.

Hospitals wouldn't let her work as a doctor. Instead, she opened her own hospital. It opened in 1857. Later, she added a women's medical college. She returned to England to work with Florence Nightingale. She worked until the age of 86. She left a very important mark on the medical profession!

Medicine Becomes Science

During Hippocrates' time, doctors were highly respected in Greece. Women could not become doctors, though. Many women worked as midwives or nurses.

Some doctors worked in private practice. They charged a lot for their services. The state paid doctors to treat the poor. It was a way to keep disease under control. It also improved public health.

Some people lied. They said they were doctors. They wanted to get paid well. They also wanted the respect people gave to doctors. This inspired Hippocrates to write a code of **ethics** for doctors.

Hippocrates was thought to be the greatest doctor of his time. He did not believe the gods were to blame for illnesses. He did not believe the superstitions. His medicine was based on looking at the body. He believed illness had a logical explanation.

Well Paid

Doctors are well paid in the United States. In 2006, the average emergency room doctor made almost $200,000 in his or her first year. You must study for many years to become a doctor.

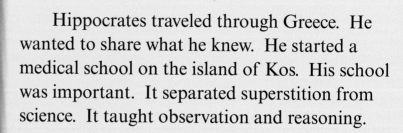

Hippocrates traveled through Greece. He wanted to share what he knew. He started a medical school on the island of Kos. His school was important. It separated superstition from science. It taught observation and reasoning.

Hippocrates believed in "learning by doing." He kept records of his patients. He noted their illnesses and their treatments. He kept track of what worked and what didn't. He learned from his experiences. He shared his learning with others. His students worked with him. They followed him when he saw his patients. They learned by doing, too.

Doctors often make difficult decisions. They must have ethics when making their decisions. Hippocrates suggested rules for doctors to follow. He was the first to do so. Later, a doctor named Galen summed up Hippocrates' rules as, "*Primum non nocere*" (PREE-mum non no-CHAIR-ay). This means, "First, do no harm!" Doctors today are held to this challenge.

Doctor Charts

Doctors still take notes about their patients. They write in a chart each time they see someone. This reminds them of the patient's medical history. Some people see the same doctor for many years. They'll have a thick chart. Today, many charts and files are being stored on computers.

Hippocratic Oath

The Hippocratic Oath reads in part as follows:

I swear by Apollo the Physician . . . and all the gods and goddesses that . . .

I will carry out, according to the best of my ability and judgment, this oath and covenant . . .

I will, according to my ability and judgment, prescribe such treatment for my patients as may be most beneficial to them and do no harm . . .

I will maintain the purity and integrity of both my life and my profession . . .

I will abstain from all intentional wrongdoing and any harm, especially from abusing the body of man or woman, bond or free.

I WILL USE TREATMENT TO HELP THE SICK ACCORDING TO MY ABILITY AND JUDGEMENT BUT NEVER WITH A VIEW TO INJURY AND WRONGDOING

HIPPOCRATIC OATH 1.

People do not agree whether Hippocrates wrote the Hippocratic Oath. They do agree on one thing, though. The oath is based on his teachings. Doctors today still follow the oath. It is often recited at medical school graduations. The oath details a patient's right to privacy. Doctors swear to lead a life of honor. They promised to treat only those who need it.

Hippocrates wrote about patient **confidentiality**. He thought patients had a right to keep things private. Doctors should not tell other people things about their patients. Doctors still practice this today. The only people who should know are the patient and others who are treating the patient.

Doctors Keep Quiet

Doctors do not tell other people about their patients' problems.

A statue of Hippocrates is found in many medical schools around the world.

Ann Preston (1813–1872)

Ann Preston was born in Pennsylvania. When her mother became sick, she returned home to take care of her younger brothers and sisters.

Preston started to see that women did not know about their own bodies. She studied the subject. Then she started teaching hygiene to women and girls. When she was 34, she started her medical studies. She worked for a doctor for two years. She applied to medical school. None would take her because she was a woman.

A medical school for women opened in Philadelphia. She entered in 1850. Three years later, she was teaching there. She later became the first female dean of the college. She helped start medical outreach. Students would go into the community. They would teach about the body and hygiene.

Preston raised enough money to open a women's hospital in 1862. She wanted women students to get medical experience. Many people didn't want women to be doctors. Preston stayed strong, though. If women would be patients, shouldn't they also be doctors? People started to see things her way. Other schools started admitting women, too.

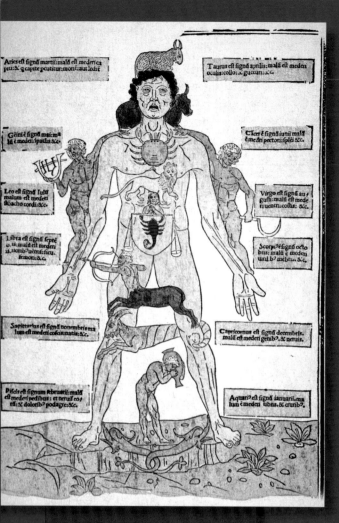

Hippocrates believed the goal of medicine should be to build a patient's strength. He believed surgery was a last resort. It should be used only when necessary. This was different from what other doctors were doing. Most practiced diagnosing and labeling the diseases. They ignored the patient.

Hippocrates was aware of **heredity**. In his writings, he noted how symptoms could appear through a family. He also noted they could appear in a community over many generations.

Not all of Hippocrates' ideas were right. He wrote that it was important for his students to study **astrology**. Medical astrology claims that body parts and diseases are linked with the sun, moon, and planets. They are also linked with the different signs of the zodiac. Hippocrates' ideas about astrology have since been thrown out.

Medicine and Astrology

In medical astrology, the nervous system is linked with the signs of Gemini and Virgo. The skeletal system is linked with Capricorn. The heart and chest are linked with Leo.

Hippocrates Said

"He who does not understand astrology is not a doctor but a fool."

Rosalyn Sussman Yalow (1921–)

Rosalyn Sussman was born in New York City. She learned to read before starting kindergarten. She went to the library every week. She loved math and science. She graduated from Hunter College, a college for women, in 1941. Sussman took a job as a secretary after graduation. She worked for a biochemist. She didn't stay there long. She was offered a job as an assistant teacher of physics at the University of Illinois. She was the only woman among 400 faculty members in her department! She soon married a man she worked with, Aaron Yalow. Two years later, she earned her Ph.D. She is a medical physicist.

Yalow helped to start a **radioisotope** service. It can measure tiny amounts of substances in blood. It was first used to study diabetes.

Yalow received a Nobel Prize in 1977. In her acceptance speech she challenged future scientists. She said that they should "work together . . . so that your world will be better than ours and the world of your children even better."

Hippocrates Leaves His Legacy

Hippocrates told doctors to take notes about their patients. They should write down how they treated each patient. They should also note how the patient responded. These notes should be passed on to other doctors.

In his writings, Hippocrates stated that medicine is not philosophy. It should be practiced on a case-by-case basis.

Hippocrates taught doctors how to work out what is wrong with a patient. He said they should first observe a patient. Then they could **diagnose** (DIE-ag-knows), or name the problem. After that, they could make a **prognosis** (PROG-no-sis), or what is likely to happen. They should observe the patient over time. They should look to see if there are any changes. Then they could treat the patient. This teaching led to the steps used in modern medicine. It is called clinical observation.

Ripe Old Age
Hippocrates died in 337 B.C. at the age of 93.

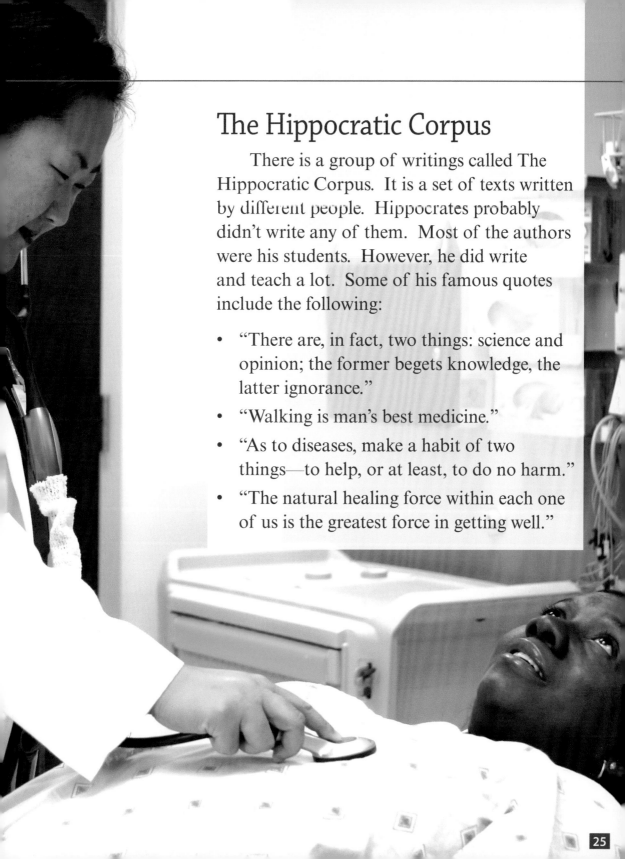

The Hippocratic Corpus

There is a group of writings called The Hippocratic Corpus. It is a set of texts written by different people. Hippocrates probably didn't write any of them. Most of the authors were his students. However, he did write and teach a lot. Some of his famous quotes include the following:

- "There are, in fact, two things: science and opinion; the former begets knowledge, the latter ignorance."
- "Walking is man's best medicine."
- "As to diseases, make a habit of two things—to help, or at least, to do no harm."
- "The natural healing force within each one of us is the greatest force in getting well."

Surgeon: Susan Love

The Dr. Susan Love Research Foundation

Ms. Fix It

Susan Love became a surgeon because she enjoyed working with her hands and wanted to help others. "I liked the idea of fixing people," she says.

When she started her career, some doctors didn't want to send their male patients to a female surgeon. They sent only female patients to Love. That didn't stop her.

Love took time to listen and talk to her patients. Some of the women she saw had breast cancer. Over time, Love became a national expert on treating the disease.

Love's patients inspired her. Many were eager to make their own decisions instead of only relying on their doctor's advice. So Love wrote a book to share what she knew. It is considered the best resource on breast cancer available.

Love spends a lot of time teaching people about breast cancer. Previously, many people didn't want to talk about it. "It's been a great reward to change the way that people look at breast cancer," Love says. "I love my work."

Lab: The Nose Knows

You will test several people to see if their abilities to smell are equal. Be sure there are no distractions. Ask yourself, is the sense of smell more developed in some people? Or are people who seem to have good noses just more focused?

Materials

- five or more volunteers
  (more volunteers give your experiment better results)
- blindfolds for the volunteers
- three or four fragrant items (such as perfume, scented soap, hot popcorn, flowers, warm brownies, garlic, a sliced orange)
- stopwatch or timer
- chart
- pen or pencil

Procedure

1 Find a room in which to conduct your experiment. Make this room as quiet as possible. Turn off radios, televisions, and other noisemakers. Close windows. Turn off anything that affects the airflow in the room (air conditioners, furnaces, etc.).

2 Blindfold your volunteers. Then lead them into the room, two at a time. Place them each about ten feet from the doorway. Set them in a comfortable position. Tell them to keep quiet and relax.

3 Tell the volunteers to quietly raise their hands whenever they smell a new item. Tell them to think about what the smell may be.

4 Have your charting materials ready. If possible have an assistant record your results.

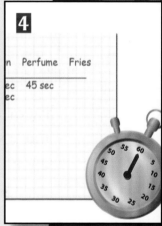

5 Bring the first item into the room and place it just inside the doorway. Spray the bottle if necessary.

6 Record the amount of time that passes before each hand is raised, in seconds. Wait until both volunteers have raised their hands. Ask them to identify the smell. Record their answers.

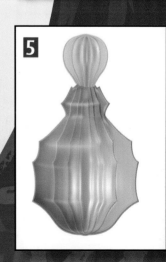

7 Repeat steps 5 and 6, using different items. Vary the time between smells. Try to "trick" them to be sure they are accurately reporting smells.

8 Repeat the test with additional volunteers. Record the results.

Glossary

anatomy—the scientific study of the body and how its parts are arranged

astrology—the study of the movements and positions of the sun, moon, planets, and stars, and the skill of describing the expected effect that these are believed to have on the character and behavior of humans

bile—a bitter yellow liquid produced by the liver that helps to digest fat

confidentiality—done or communicated in confidence

diagnose—to figure out what is wrong with a patient

dissection—to cut apart or separate tissue, especially for anatomical study

epilepsy—a condition of the brain that causes a person to lose consciousness for short periods or to move in a violent and uncontrolled way

ethics—a system of accepted beliefs that control behavior, especially such a system based on morals

heredity—the process by which characteristics are given from a parent to their child through the parents' genes

humors—one of the four bodily fluids: blood, phlegm, yellow bile, and black bile

Nobel Prize—an award given annually for outstanding contributions to society

organ—a body part that has a specific role or job, such as the heart

pasteurization—heating a drink or other food to kill microorganisms that could cause disease, spoiling, or unwanted fermentation

penicillin—a type of medicine that kills bacteria; an antibiotic

phlegm—a thick mucus that is produced especially when you have a cold

pneumonia—a serious illness in which one or both lungs become red and swollen and filled with liquid

prognosis—a doctor's judgment of the likely or expected development of a disease or of the chances of getting better

radioisotope—a naturally or artificially produced isotope of an element

Index

Sally Ride Science

Sally Ride Science™ is an innovative content company dedicated to fueling young people's interests in science. Our publications and programs provide opportunities for students and teachers to explore the captivating world of science—from astrobiology to zoology. We bring science to life and show young people that science is creative, collaborative, fascinating, and fun.

Image Credits

Cover: Visual Arts Library (London)/Alamy; p.3 Olga Shelego/Shutterstock; p.4 (top) Yan Vugenfirer/Shutterstock; p.4 (left) Mary Evans Picture Library/Alamy; p.4 (bottom) Sheila Terry/Photo Researchers, Inc.; p.5 Visual Arts Library/Alamy; p.6 (top) Photos.com; p.6 (bottom) Tim Bradley; pp.6–7 Paul Cowan/Shutterstock; p.7 Nick Belton/iStockphoto; p.8 (left) Olga Shelego/Shutterstock; p.8 (bottom) A. E. Knost/Shutterstock; pp.8–9 Tim Bradley; p.9 David Riley/Alamy; p.10 (top) Maksim Shmeljov/Shutterstock; p.10 (left) Juriah Mosin/Shutterstock; pp.10–11 Shawn Pecor/Shutterstock; p.11 Medical-on-Line/Alamy; p.11 (back) Ttphoto/Shutterstock; p.12 The Granger Collection, New York; pp.12–13 Mary Evans Picture Library/Alamy; p.13 (bottom) Kelvin Kho/Shutterstock; p.14 (top) paulaphoto/Shutterstock; p.14 (bottom) Godfer/Dreamstime.com; pp.14–15 North Wind Picture Archives/Alamy; p.15 (bottom) Ron Hilton/Shutterstock; p.16 (top) The Museum of the City of New York/Getty Images; p.17 (bottom) Jaimie Duplass/Shutterstock; p.18 (top) Elena Elisseeva/Shutterstock; p.18 (left) Cristian Teichner/Shutterstock; p.19 Yan Vugenfirer/Shutterstock; p.19 (right) Tony Lilley/Alamy; p.20 POPPERFOTO/Alamy; p.21 Rick Reason; p.21 (bottom) Tim Bradley; p.22 The Granger Collection, New York; p.23 The Granger Collection, New York; p.24 (top) PhotoCreate/Shutterstock; p.24 (bottom) Mary Evans Picture Library/Alamy; p.25 Andrew Gentry/Shutterstock; p.28 (top) Robyn Mackenzie/Shutterstock; pp.28–29 Nicolle Rager Fuller; p.32 Getty Images